---

6 Steps To 6 Figures

THE BIG BOSS GUIDE

BY
SHAKIRA BURTON

Copyright © 2022 by **Shakira Burton**
All rights reserved. This book or any portion thereof
may not be reproduced or used in any manner whatsoever without the
express written permission of the publisher except for the use of brief
quotations in a book review.

Printed in the United States of America

First Edition, 2022
PAPERBACK ISBN 978-1-0880-3277-0
E-BOOK ISBN 978-1-0880-3278-7

Red Pen Edits and Consulting, LLC
P. O. Box 25283
Columbia, SC 29223
www.redpeneditsllc.com

TABLE OF CONTENTS

DEDICATIONS	1
INTRODUCTION	2
What Does It Mean To Be A BoSS?	
CHAPTER 1	5
Mission Statements And Corporate Objectives	
CHAPTER 2	8
Define Your Audience	
CHAPTER 3	11
Setting SMART Goals	
CHAPTER 4	15
Develop A Budget	
CHAPTER 5	18
5 P's of Marketing	
CHAPTER 6	24
Put Your Plans In Action And Monitor Your Results!	
ABOUT THE AUTHOR	27

DEDICATIONS

This book is dedicated to anyone that wants to step out on faith and become their own BO$$!

-Nothing is impossible. The word itself is I'M POSSIBLE!

Use the word impossible to your advantage by changing it to I'M POSSIBLE!

INTRODUCTION

What Does It Mean To Be A Boss?

When I came up with the thought of becoming my own boss, I got excited with the fact of working for myself and doing things how and when I'd like. My purpose for going into business for myself was because I like to set the rules for myself and come up with my own creative ideas. Even if you're not in a creative field, being your own boss allows you to flex your creative muscles on a daily basis. You can try out new strategies and find ways to make your business better. Being able to have the ability and power to make my own financial decisions regarding my business is what motivated me to start and keep going. The business itself is valuable and I can set my own salary. No more waiting on a raise or even waiting to get paid. While most jobs you drag yourself out of bed to go to, I found a bit of peace in becoming my own boss. It's a job that's guaranteed to make you smile and you work in your own comfortable place. You choose the overall direction of your business, which means you're more likely to be happy with the work in the first place. Taking on the responsibilities of running a business is scary! But it also offers some pretty terrific rewards. Many of us have dreamed about it, but few of us really take the leap. Isn't it time you started your own business and control your own professional destiny?

What Does Being A Boss Mean To You?

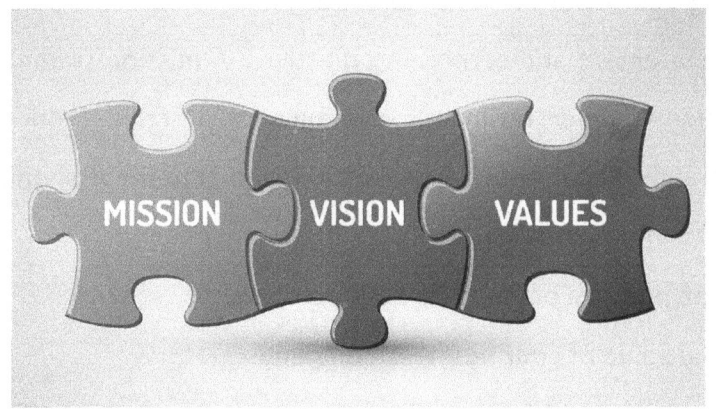

CHAPTER 1

Mission Statements And Corporate Objectives

When starting a business, there are many things you should know. When I started my business, I didn't know everything from the beginning. Now, that I have some business experience (also known as sweat in the game), I am in a position to pass on the knowledge. One of the first steps to becoming your own boss is to look out for your business by creating a mission statement and corporate objectives. A mission statement is an explanation of your business's existence. It describes your business purpose and overall intentions. Your mission statement should always include 3 components:

- the purpose of your business/company
- the value of your business/company
- and the goal for your business/company.

When making your business' mission statement, be sure to keep your statement short and understanding. A corporate objective is a goal or outcome that you want your business to achieve. Each objective for your business should be focused on important aspects of your business. It is recommended that you do not set too many objectives, or you could risk losing focus. Mission statements and corporate objectives are important because they help to provide a more precise understanding of how you will run your business. It helps to outline your company's direction and gives your employees clear objectives. A mission statement can be a simple statement or a full document. Ultimately, it helps when making decisions, developing strategies and performing day to day tasks.

What Is The Mission For Your Business Idea?

CHAPTER 2

Define Your Audience

In this chapter, we will find out how to find your audience. Your audience is also known as your target market or customer base. It is imperative to DEFINE your audience when starting a business. Defining your audience means that you search for all the right customers that may like what you sell. When defining your audience, think about who you're trying to reach with your service/product. First, you must determine what is trending and popular to the audience that you hope to offer your product or service. Then, describe your ideal customer. Where will you reach them? In stores? On social media? Who are they? Are they male or female? Are they young or old? Depending on the type of business that you setup, you may be able to serve both demographics. You want to educate yourself on the buying habits of your potential customer. Why do they buy what they buy? Do they buy based on how the product or service can benefit them? Most consumers purchase things that they need. As the business owner, you must determine all of the factors that attribute to the buying patterns of your potential customer. Lastly, you must consider how your potential customer prefers to pay. Some people still like cash transactions, but in this new virtual world, there are multiple methods to accept payment such as CashApp, PayPal, Venmo, and Zelle just to name a few. It is suggested that you explore all payment method options and make them available on your website.

Who Is Your Target Market/Audience?

Age?   Race?   Financial Status?   Demographic?

_____
_____
_____
_____
_____
_____
_____
_____
_____
_____
_____
_____

CHAPTER 3

Setting SMART goals

Goal setting is essential to the success of any business. In 1981, George T. Doran established an acronym for S.M.A.R.T. as a means to assist decision makers with setting feasible goals. S.M.A.R.T. stands for specific, measurable, attainable, realistic and time related. Specific goals must be clear and well defined. Goals must be measurable. Measuring your goals' success will assist you with celebrating progress based on benchmarks and milestones. Setting attainable goals for your business allows you to delegate responsibilities through your business towards a common goal. Realistic goals are goals that you know you can achieve with the proper allotment of resources. Goals should cause you to expand on your abilities without stressing you out. Time bound goals give you a deadline to accomplish steps towards the ultimate goal. Setting deadlines will create a sense of urgency in making sure the goal is accomplished. In all of this goal setting, you should practice writing down your goals and placing them in visible areas that will remind you of things you want to see happen in your personal and business lives.

Goal Setting

Goals	**S**pecific?	**M**easurable?	**A**ttainable?	**R**ealistic?	**T**ime-bound?

What More Can Be Done To Make Your Goals S.M.A.R.T?

CHAPTER 4

Develop A Budget

It is a proven fact that most businesses fail in the first five years of existence for multiple reasons. One of the main reasons that they fail is due to a lack of financial preparedness. Financial planning and business budgeting is necessary for the success of a business. To become a BOSS, you must determine the amount of income that you expect from your business. Everything in your business depends on profit and loss. We all want to be successful in business, but what is the quantitative value of your business' success. You must know your income and how much expenses your business will incur. Most entrepreneurs still work a 9-5 job and they use some of that income to fund their business. Once you learn the numbers, it will help you maintain a budget for your business. Budgeting for your business includes gathering your financial paperwork, calculating your monthly income and expenses, determining your fixed and variable expenses, and finally making adjustments that will benefit your business. Budgeting for your business is one of the hardest tasks in the business building process. When it comes to making money, you must be wise and strive to make BOSS moves!

BO$$ Budget

Expected Income	Costs	Frequency

Expected Expenses	Costs	Frequency

CHAPTER 5

5 P's of Marketing

The 5 P's of marketing create a great framework of strategies to use when starting a business. The 5 P's are product, price, place, promotion, and people. Below, you will find inquisitions into each P and an explanation for further knowledge.

P - Product

The first "P" is Product. What products or services do you provide? Be specific. What are some the expected outcomes of using the product or the details of the services you provide? Explain the features of your products and services and how they specifically benefit your market.

It's also important to identify how your products or services differ from what your competitors offer. This is also known as a competitive advantage. Understand how your product solves your market's problem in a way that is different from your competition is crucial.

P - Price

The 2nd "P" is Price. What are you charging for your product or service? Be sure it's enough to cover all of your expenses and make a profit. It also needs to fit what your market is willing to pay. Be sure to do your research to find out what your competitors are charging and figure out where you'd like to fit in on the spectrum. Include any discounts or sales you may have going on as well.

P - Place

The 3rd "P" is Place. Where are your products and services being sold? How are your products and services distributed? How will you get them to your customers and clients? For example, if you have a local order, you could offer delivery to your services with an additional fee. If an order needs to be shipped, you could offer free shipping based on the shipping carrier in your fees.

P - Promotion

The 4th "P" is promotion. What methods are you currently or planning to use to announce your product/services to your target market/audience? Be sure to understand your market, including where it can be found and how you can create marketing messages that will appeal to your audience. On some social media platforms, you can pay for promotions to gain more recognition.

P - People

The final "P" is for People. Who is helping you in your business? The people and services that you use in your business can impact your success. If you or any of your personnel are rude, you could lose customers and clients. Customers have a choice with whom they do business. They prefer companies that provide customer service that is attentive and responsive to their needs and provide user-friendly systems. Happy customers will become repeated customers and refer new business.

Identify The P's Of Your Marketing Mix

P - What Is Your Product/Service?

_____

_____

_____

P - What Is Your Price?

_____

_____

_____

P - Where Is Your Place?

_____

_____

_____

P - What Is Your Promotion?

_____

_____

_____

P - Who Are Your People?

_____

_____

_____

CHAPTER 6

Put Your Plans In Action And Monitor Your Results!

Drive Your Organization With A Big Vision

Identify your business objectives and define what you hope to accomplish.

Establish Big Goals

Come up with big goals that you've determined for your business to achieve and make your dreams come true.

Celebrate Wins

Celebrating wins helps you remember the goals you set and why you set them. All your hard work is going to pay off and celebrating each goal makes you want to do more.

Seek Out New Ideas

Experiment with 'maybe' ideas. If you find a new idea that you're comfortable with, do your research. If possible, get a sample. If you're satisfied with the quality, go for it!

Ignore Distractions

Ignore anything that may cause you to lose focus. Distractions turn into procrastination which causes you to lose track of what it will take for your business to be successful. Ignoring and eliminating distractions will set you on track for positive results.

Empower Through Ownership

Set clear expectations. Accept ideas and inputs.

Be Passionate

"Passion is the fuel that entrepreneurs need to keep going." Love what you do and NEVER give up. Put yourself in position to achieve the vision. The more passionate that the entrepreneur is about the vision, the more likely they are to succeed.

ABOUT THE AUTHOR
~ SHAKIRA BURTON ~

Shakira Burton is a full-time mother of 2, owner of 3 businesses, and manager of her children's business, The Kidz Customz and Boutique LLC. She graduated from Richland Northeast High School (Columbia, SC) in 2014 and aspires to complete the Fire Academy in 2023. The entrepreneurial seed was planted in 2017 when she had the initial thought to work for herself. While working at Lowe's in 2018, Shakira had her first son. From that moment, she sought methods to be her own boss. Her dream has always been to create a legacy wherein her children would walk in her footsteps. In March of 2019. Shakira launched her first business, Golden Apparel LLC, an all-women's clothing boutique. The year of 2020 was filled with more knowledge, recognition and two significant births: her daughter and her second business, Pure Beauty Skincare, a natural skincare line for men and women.

Her most recent project is the creation of her third business, My Own Boss Academy, and the release of her debut book. Her inspiration to write this book came from constant questions from aspiring and like-minded entrepreneurs. Many inquired about how she started multiple businesses and what attributes to her continual motivation. Shakira remembered how she launched into business without guidance and deemed it necessary to share from her knowledge and expertise to help future entrepreneurs become more successful in business

"The dream is free. The hustle is sold separately." - George Koufalis

Follow Shakira On Facebook:
Shakira LaPrincia Ajee

Follow Shakira On Instagram:
@x_laprinciaajee

Email:
myownbossacademy2022@gmail.com

CPSIA information can be obtained
at www.ICGtesting.com
Printed in the USA
LVHW080918180522
719028LV00032BB/1393